Contents

These super-sized scenes act as a wonderful focal point for your class. Look for the vocabulary in the scene together. You might want to point to more vocabulary in the scene. A full list of words starting with the target sound can be found at the bottom of each page.

Page	Letter	Character name	Key vocabulary words
2	a	Annie Apple	apple, ant, arrow
4	b	Bouncy Ben	book, ball, boat
6	c	Clever Cat	car, cup, cake
8	d	Dippy Duck	dog, drum, dad
10	e	Eddy Elephant	egg, envelope, elbow
12	f	Firefighter Fred	fish, frog, fire
14	g	Golden Girl	garden, gate, grass
16	h	Harry Hat Man	hat, house, hand
18	i	Impy Ink	in, ink, insect
20	j	Jumping Jim	jet, juice, jam
22	k	Kicking King	key, kettle, kitchen
24	l	Lucy Lamp Light	leg, log, lion
26	m	Munching Mike	map, milk, man
28	n	Noisy Nick	nine, nose, noodles
30	o	Oscar Orange	on, off, orange
32	p	Peter Puppy	pen, paint, pencil
34	q	Quarrelsome Queen	quarter, question, quilt
36	r	Red Robot	rain, river, rice
38	s	Sammy Snake	sun, sea, sand
40	t	Talking Tess	table, toys, ten
42	u	Uppy Umbrella	up, under, umbrella
44	v	Vicky Violet	van, vegetables, vet
46	w	Walter Walrus	water, watch, window
48	x	Fix-it Max	six, box, fox
50	y	Yellow Yo-yo Man	yellow, yo-yo, yogurt
52	z	Zig Zag Zebra	zero, zip, zoo
54	Long a	Mr A, the Apron Man	acorn, alien, apron
56	Long e	Mr E, the Easy Magic Man	eagle, east, eat
58	Long i	Mr I, the Ice Cream Man	iron, ice cream, island
60	Long o	Mr O, the Old Man	ocean, open, old
62	Long u	Mr U, the Uniform Man	unicorn, unicycle, uniform

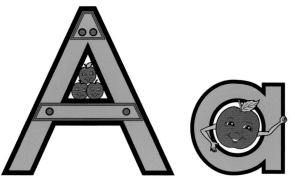

This is Annie Apple.
She says, a.

apple

ant

arrow

Extra vocabulary to find in the scene:
acrobat, alligator, animals, ankles, anteater, antelope, apple trees, atlas, axe

 This is Bouncy Ben.
He says, b.

book

ball

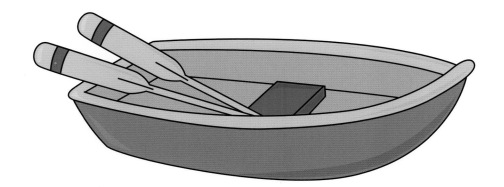

boat

Extra vocabulary to find in the scene: back, balloon, bat, bee, blackberries, bluebells, bluetit, box, branch, bridge, brothers, brown, bulrushes, bushes, buttercups, butterfly

5

  This is Clever Cat.
She says, c.

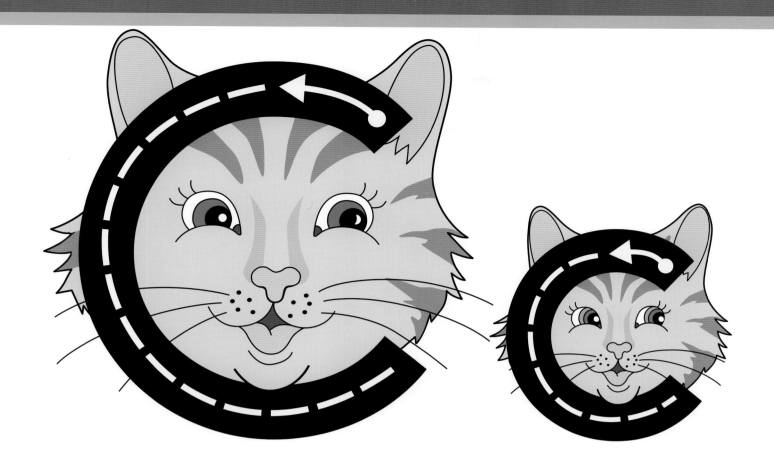

car

cup

cake

Extra vocabulary to find in the scene:
calf, carrot, castle, cat, caterpillar, clouds, cocoa, cottage, cow, crocus, crossword, crows, cucumber

 This is Dippy Duck.
She says, d.

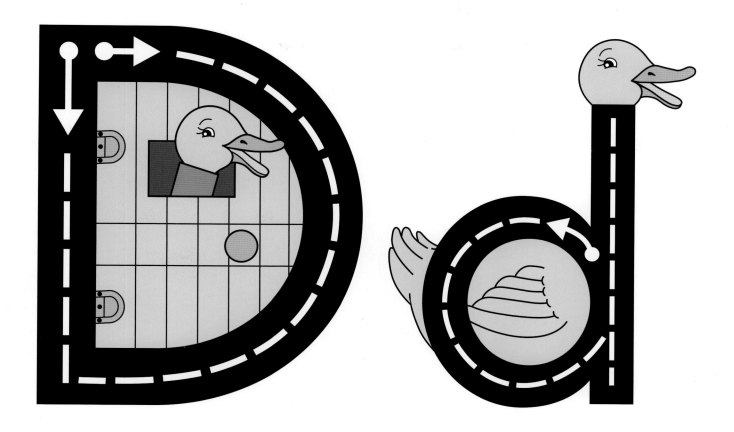

dog

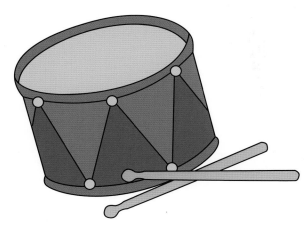

drum

dad

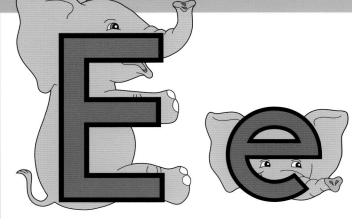

This is Eddy Elephant.
He says, e.

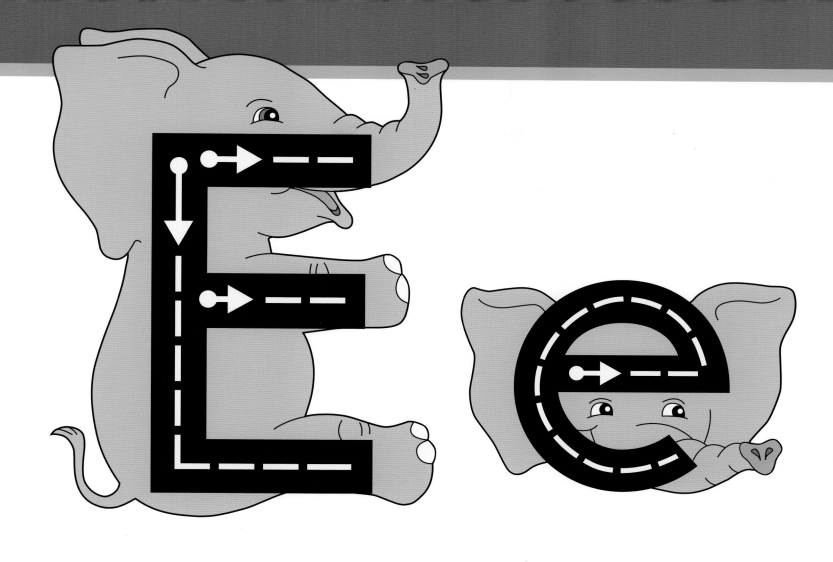

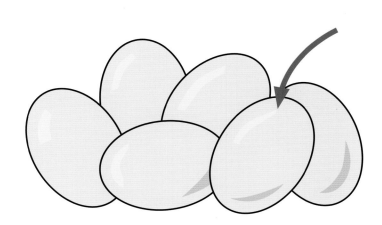

egg

elbow

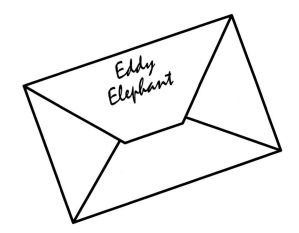

envelope

Extra vocabulary to find in the scene: Ecuador, edges, eggplant, elephant, emerald, enchiladas, entrance, escalator, Estonia, exercise equipment, exit

11

This is Firefighter Fred.

He says, f.

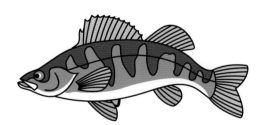

fish

frog

fire

Extra vocabulary to find in the scene:
farm, fence, fern, fir trees, fire engine, five, flag, flames, flowers, foam, forest, four, fox

13

This is Golden Girl.
She says, g.

garden

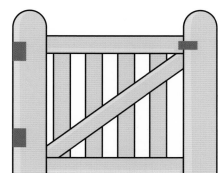

gate

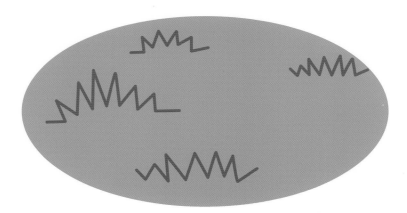

grass

Extra vocabulary to find in the scene:
goat, goose, gladioli, glass, glasses, grapes, green, greenhouse

This is Harry Hat Man.

He says, h.

hat house

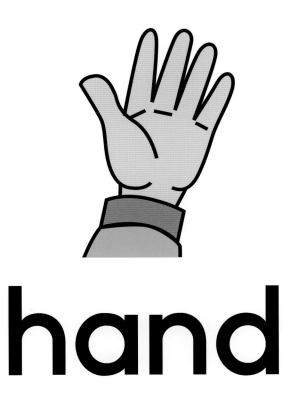

hand

Extra vocabulary to find in the scene: hair, hay, head, hedge, hedgehogs, heels, helicopter, hen, hill, hives, home, horse, hut, hydrangea

17

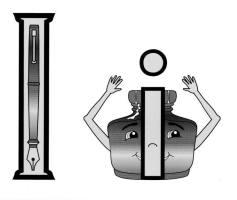

This is Impy Ink.
He says, i.

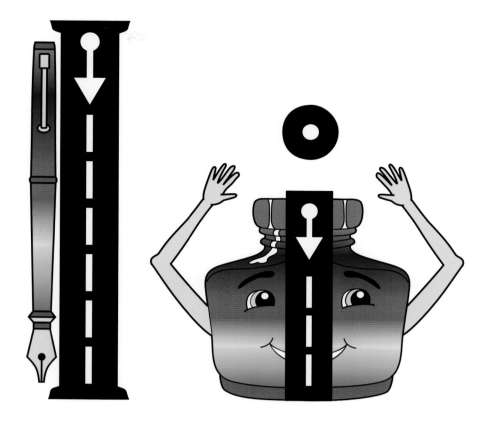

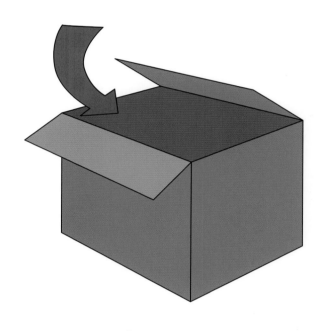

in

ink

insect

This is Jumping Jim.

He says, j.

jam

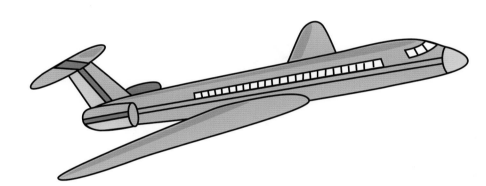

jet

juice

 This is Kicking King.
He says, k.

key

kettle

kitchen

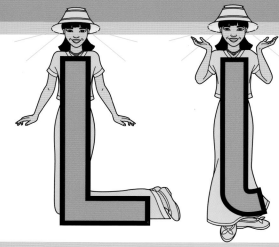 This is Lucy Lamp Light.

She says, l.

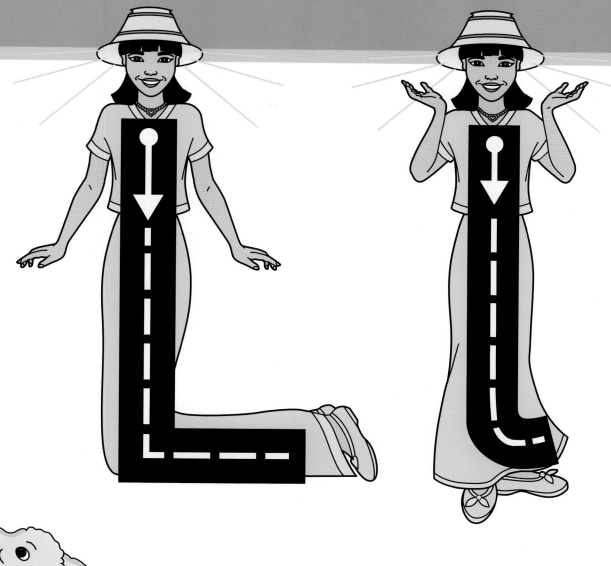

leg

log

lion

Extra vocabulary to find in the scene: ladder, lamb, leaves, lemons, leopard, light, lighthouse, lilies, lion cub, lizard, llama, lobster, lorry

25

 This is Munching Mike.

He says, m.

map

milk

man

Extra vocabulary to find in the scene: magnet, magpie, mango, marshmallows, melon, metal, meteor, midnight, millipede, monkey, moon, moose, mountains, mushrooms

27

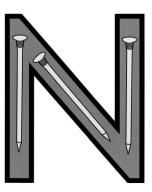  This is Noisy Nick.
He says, n.

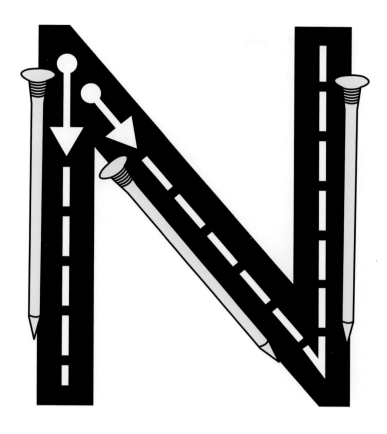

nine

nose

noodles

This is Oscar Orange.
He says, o.

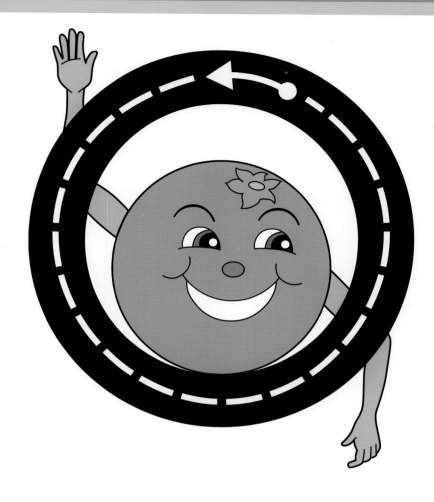

on

off

orange

This is Peter Puppy.
He says, p.

pen

paint

pencil

Extra vocabulary to find in the scene: palm tree, paper, park, path, peaches, pears, penguin, pigeons, pineapple, pink, pool, poppies, present, purple

33

 This is Quarrelsome Queen. She says, qu.

quarter

quilt

question

This is Red Robot.
He says, r.

rain

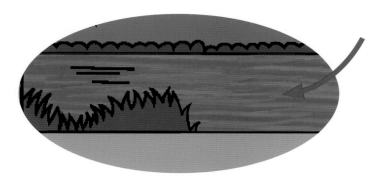

river

rice

Extra vocabulary to find in the scene: rabbit, raccoon, radio, rainbow, recorder, red, remote control, rider, robin, roller skates, rose, rubbish, ruler

37

 This is Sammy Snake.
He says, s.

sun

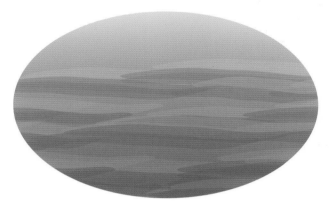

sea

sand

Extra vocabulary: sail boat, sandwich, saucer, seagull, seaweed, six, sky, seven socks, starfish, stones, strawberries, sun cream, sundae, sunglasses, sunhat, swimming pool

 This is Talking Tess.
She says, t.

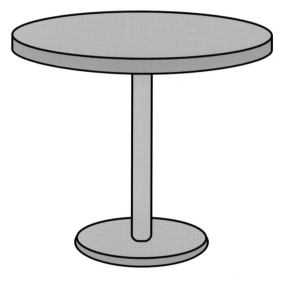

table

toys

10
ten

Extra vocabulary to find in the scene: teddy, telephone, toad, toes, tortoise, towers, town, train, trees, tricycle, trousers, t-shirt, tulips, tyres

This is Uppy Umbrella.

She says, u.

up

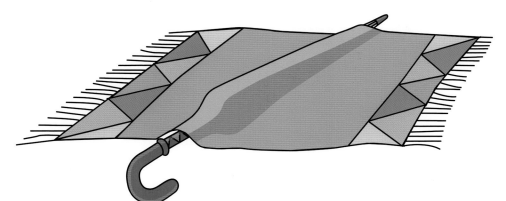

under

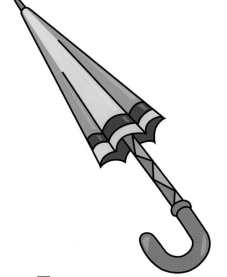

umbrella

 This is Vicky Violet.
She says, v.

van

vet

vegetables

This is Walter Walrus.

He says, w.

watch   **water**

window

Extra vocabulary to find in the scene:
wasp, waves, well, whiskers, white, windmill, wind turbines, wolf, wombat, woodpecker, worms

47

This is Fix-it Max.
He says, x.

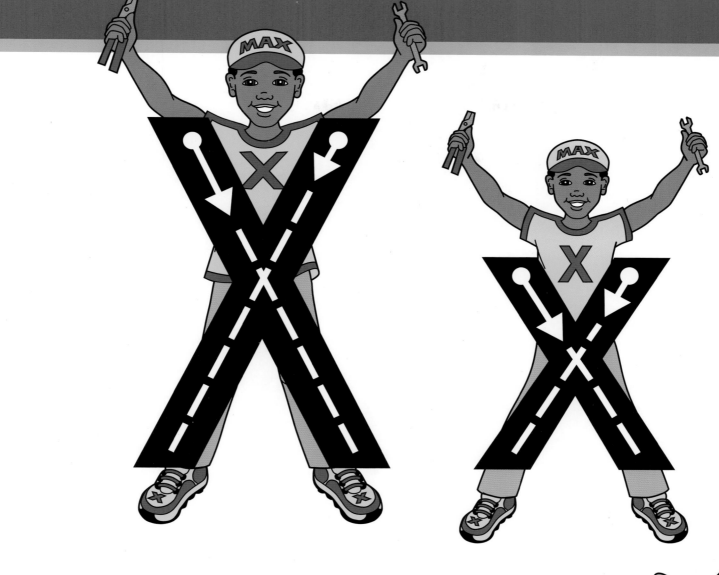

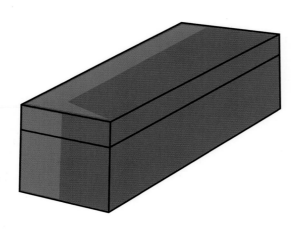

box   fox

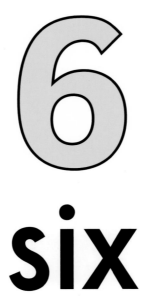

six

This is Yellow Yo-yo Man.

He says, y.

yellow

yogurt

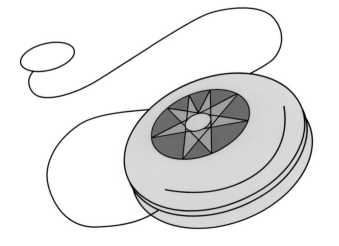

yo-yo

This is Zig Zag Zebra.
She says, z.

0 **zero**

zip

zoo

Extra vocabulary to find in the scene:
zebra, zookeeper, zoom lens (camera)

This is Mr A, the Apron Man.

He says his name, a.

acorn

alien

apron

This is Mr E, the Easy Magic Man. He says his name, e.

eagle

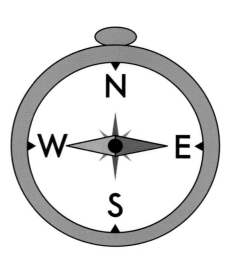

east

eat

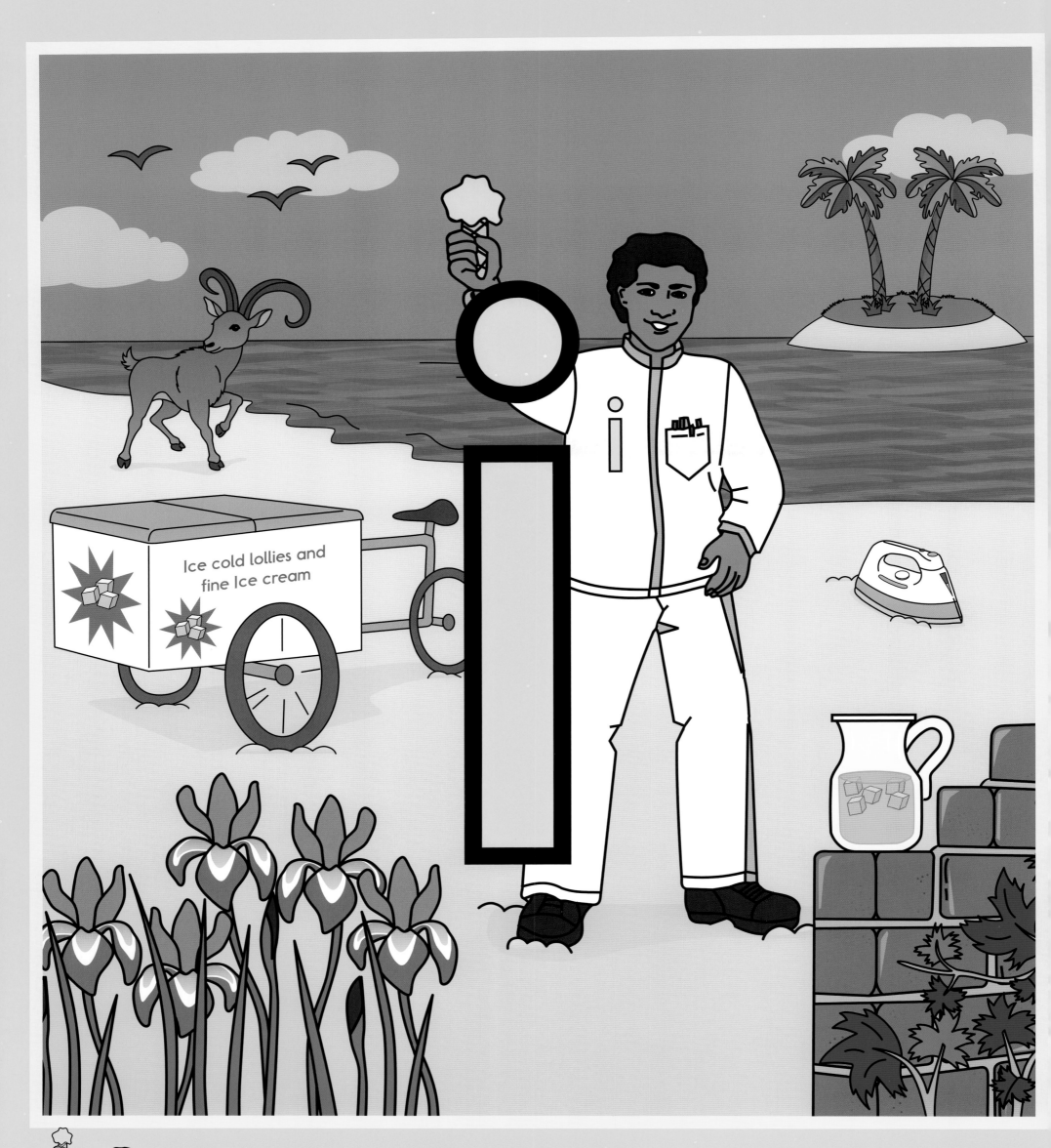

Ice cold lollies and
fine Ice cream

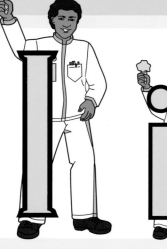

This is Mr I, the Ice Cream Man.

He says his name, i.

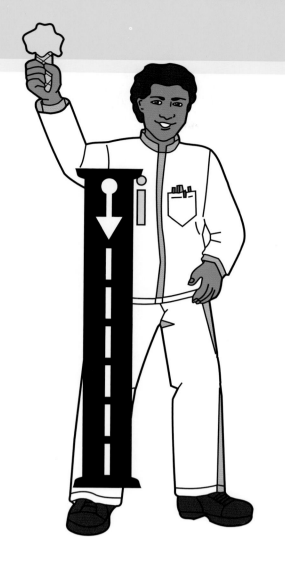
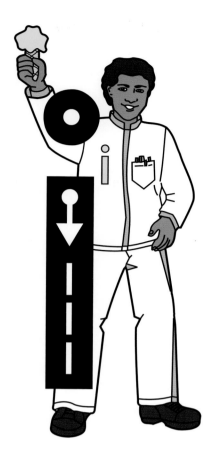

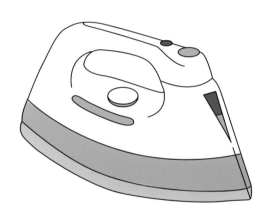

iron

island

ice cream

This is Mr O, the Old Man.

He says his name, o.

ocean

old

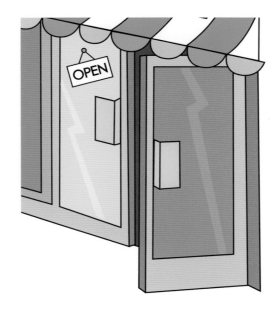

open

Extra vocabulary to find in the scene:
oak (decking), oat biscuits, oboe, ocean liner (boat) overcast (sky), oval (table), overalls

61

Get ready for University

Explore the Universe

Useful University Tips

How to use Utensils

The United Kingdom

The United States of America

The United States of America

Utensils

School uniform

 This is Mr U, the Uniform Man. He says his name, u.

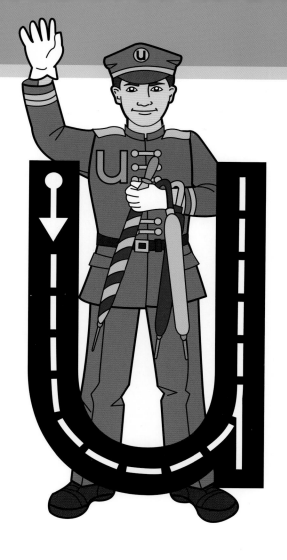

unicorn unicycle

uniform

a-z Characters and Shapes

These short rhymes help to explain how to form the lowercase letter shapes. They are also available as songs on the *Handwriting Songs CD* or as a digital download. Uppercase songs now also available!

Annie Apple
At the leaf begin.
Go round the apple this way.
Then add a line down,
so Annie won't roll away.

Bouncy Ben
Brush down Ben's
big, long ears.
Go up and round his head
so his face appears!

Clever Cat
Curve round Clever Cat's
face to begin.
Then gently tickle her
under her chin.

Dippy Duck
Draw Dippy Duck's back.
Go round her tum.
Go up to her head.
Then down you come!

Eddy Elephant
Ed has a headband.
Draw it and then
stroke round his head
and his trunk to the end.

Firefighter Fred
First draw Fred's helmet.
Then go down a way.
Give him some arms
and he'll put out the blaze.

Golden Girl
Go round Golden Girl's head.
Go down her golden hair.
Then curve to make her swing,
so she can sit there.

Harry Hat Man
Hurry from the Hat Man's head
down to his heel on the ground.
Go up and bend his knee over.
so he'll hop while he
makes his sound.

Impy Ink
Inside the ink bottle
draw a line.
Add an inky dot.
That's fine!

Jumping Jim
Just draw down Jim,
bending his knees.
Then add the one ball
which everyone sees.

Kicking King
Kicking King's body
is a straight stick.
Add his arm, then his leg,
so he can kick!

Lucy Lamp Light
Lucy looks like one long line.
Go straight from head to foot
and she's ready to shine!

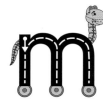

Munching Mike
Make Munching Mike's
back leg first,
then his second leg, and third,
so he can go munch-munching
in a word.

Noisy Nick
'Now bang my nail,'
Noisy Nick said.
'Go up and over
around my head.'

Oscar Orange
On Oscar Orange
start at the top.
Go all the way round him,
and... then stop.

Peter Puppy
Pat Peter Puppy properly.
First stroke down his ear,
then up and round his face
so he won't shed a tear.

Quarrelsome Queen
Quickly go round the
Queen's cross face.
Then comb her beautiful
hair into place.

Red Robot
Run down Red Robot's body.
Go up to his arm and his hand.
Then watch out for this robot
roaming round Letterland.

Sammy Snake
Start at Sam's head
where he can see.
Stroke down to his tail,
oh so care-ful-ly!

Talking Tess
Tall as a tower make
Talking Tess stand.
Go from head to toe,
and then from hand to hand.

Uppy Umbrella
Under the umbrella
draw a shape like a cup.
Then draw a straight line
so it won't tip up.

Vicky Violet
Very neatly,
start at the top.
Draw down your vase,
then up and stop.

Walter Walrus
When you draw
the Walrus' wells,
with wild and wavy water,
whizz down and up and then...,
whizz down and up again.

Fix-it Max
Fix two sticks,
to look like this.
That's how to draw
a little kiss.

Yellow Yo-yo Man
You first make the yo-yo sack
on the Yo-yo Man's back,
and then go down to his toes
so he can sell his yo-yos.

Zig Zag Zebra
Zip along Zig Zag's nose.
Stroke her neck...,
stroke her back...
Zzzoom! Away she goes.